The editors wish to thank Dora Galitzki,
plant information specialist at the New York Botanical Garden,
for her help in making this book as accurate as possible.

Copyright © 1991 by Ravensburger Buchverlag Otto Maier GmbH
All rights reserved under International and Pan-American Copyright Conventions.
Published in the United States by Random House, Inc., New York
Originally published in Germany by Ravensburger Buchverlag Otto Maier GmbH
in 1989 under the title *Gartenbuch für Kinder*
Copyright © 1989 by Ravensburger Buchverlag Otto Maier GmbH

Library of Congress Cataloging-in-Publication Data
Markmann, Erika. [Gartenbuch für Kinder. English]
Grow it! an indoor/outdoor gardening guide for kids / by Erika Markmann ; illustrated by Gisela Könemund.
p. cm. Translation of: Gartenbuch für Kinder. Includes index.
Summary: Provides tips on how to grow and care for plants.
ISBN 0-679-81528-7 (pbk.)—ISBN 0-679-91528-1 (lib. bdg.)
1. Gardening—Juvenile literature. [1. Gardening.]
I. Könemund, Gisela, ill. II. Title.
SB457.M3713 1991 635—dc20 90-45043 CIP AC

Manufactured in the United States of America 10 9 8 7 6 5 4 3 2 1

GROW IT!

An Indoor/Outdoor Gardening Guide for Kids

By Erika Markmann

Illustrated by Gisela Könemund

RANDOM HOUSE 🏠 NEW YORK

Contents

You and Your Plant: The Perfect Match

As soon as you get your plant home, give it a checkup!

Great gardeners aren't born with "green thumbs"—they have to learn about plants. You can learn too. With a little practice, you can make a beautiful garden grow just about anywhere and just about anytime. Why not turn a room into a jungle of potted plants? Or transform a terrace into a mini-farm?

It all starts with making the

These plants are easy to care for.

Spider plant   Fatsia   Cast-iron plant   Umbrella plant

Turn a room into a jungle!

right choices. If you want an indoor garden, try to choose plants that will be comfortable in your home. Is your house or apartment usually warm? Then ask the florist which plants like warm temperatures. Does the room you have in mind get only a little light? Pick plants that don't need much direct sun, such as ferns, palms, and philodendrons. And if you haven't had much gardening experience, start with very simple plants. A snake plant or a cast-iron plant, for example, won't mind much if

you put it in the wrong place or forget to water it every once in a while.

At the nursery or florist shop, you'll see rows and rows of plants. Be sure to pick the ones that stand nice and straight, have well-developed green leaves, and look healthy. If a plant has wilted leaves and is sitting in a dirty pot with very wet or very dry

Flowering plants: Choose ones with a lot of buds.

soil, don't buy it. The florist hasn't taken good care of it.

Once you do choose a healthy plant, ask for its name (try to get the Latin name too) so you can find out how to care for it and handle any problems that may come up.

Examine your plant carefully one more time when you get home. If you find a wilted leaf, pluck it off. Poke the soil with your finger, and if it feels dry, water it until water drips out of the hole in the bottom of the pot. (Put the pot on a saucer so that water doesn't flood onto your windowsill, floor, or furniture.) If the pot seems too small, move your plant to a larger pot right away (see directions for repotting, pages 20–21).

Make your own nursery for baby plants with a cardboard box and clear plastic wrap.

Just imagine spending the whole day in a dark room—ugh! Plants seem to feel the same way. If they're kept in the dark, they'll search for light by growing very long branches. But the branches will be thin and fragile instead of thick and strong.

Leaves will stay small and pale, and there won't be any blossoms.

Plants need light—but not all of them need the same amount. Cactuses, plants with thick, fleshy leaves (for instance, a snake plant), and miniature fruit trees like a lot of sun. They'll be most comfortable at a window looking south. Almost all other plants do well in bright places *without* too much sun. Too much light will make them droopy. Windows facing east or west get what

gardeners call indirect light and make a good home for most plants. Finally, there are plants that love shady places: palms, ferns, hydrangeas, and others with large, soft leaves. Put these far away from windows or near windows facing north. (Make sure to keep your plants on the indoor part of your windowsill; it can be dangerous or even illegal to put them on outside windowsills.)

Here are a couple of tricks to help your plants get the right kind of light. If there's too much sun, try moving a plant a bit farther into the room. Every inch makes a difference! During the

Let There Be Light

Make a sunshade!

Sunny

Indirect light

Shady

sunniest noon hours in the summer, you may even want to slide a newspaper between the plant and the windowpane.

If there's not enough light—a common problem in winter, when the sun doesn't shine as long every day—move your plants to the brightest window. And clean the glass, too: even a little dirt eats up light. If your windowsill isn't large enough for all your plants, a special plant light will help. You can buy one at a garden center. These lights should hang about a foot above the plant and shine for 10 hours a day.

Try this experiment to see how light changes the color of the leaves of a poinsettia. You will need a poinsettia that blossomed last year but is now only a green plant. In the fall put the plant under a cardboard box or in a very dark closet for 14 hours every night for at least six weeks. The top layer of leaves will turn red, forming a new "flower" in time for the holidays!

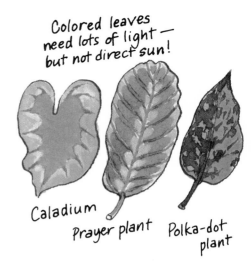

Colored leaves need lots of light—but not direct sun!

Caladium

Prayer plant

Polka-dot plant

EXPERIMENT

rrrring

DO NOT LIFT !!!

Whew! It's hot!

A lighter-colored pot would be cooler.

Cactuses get the sunniest place.

MEXICO

Plants like fresh air. If you want to be especially good to your plants, put them on the terrace or dig them into a garden bed—pots and all!—in warm weather. Leave a small space in the ground under the pot; this helps keep earthworms from crawling in through the hole in the bottom. (Worms are actually good for outdoor plants, but you don't want to bring them into the house with you when you take your plants inside.) Outside, rain will clean your plants' leaves. They'll become strong and healthy. Palm trees, ivies, and oleanders especially love fresh air. But not every plant can live outdoors: rain will ruin those with hairy leaves, like African violets.

If you don't have a place outside for your plants, open the windows and fill the indoors with fresh air. The smaller the room, the more often it should be aired. But be careful. Before you open the windows, close the door. That will keep out drafts. In a draft some sensitive plants may lose all their leaves. Air the rooms during the winter, too, but only if there is no frost outside. Some plants will freeze to death even after just a few minutes in cold air. (Something else to keep in mind: If your home is being painted or renovated, it's best to let your plants stay with

African violets stay inside.

There's Something in the Air

Some plants like to spend the summer outside.

Agave

Palm tree

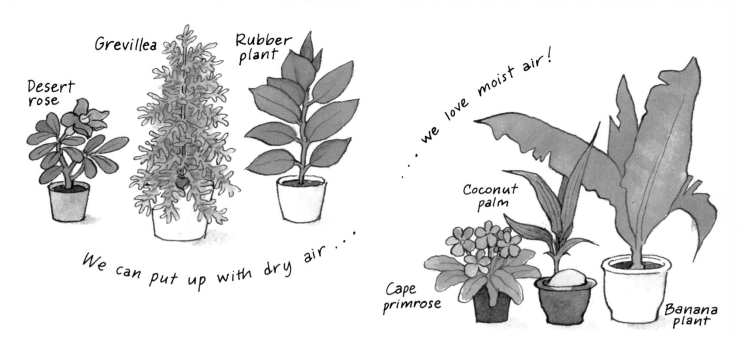

Desert rose

Grevillea

Rubber plant

We can put up with dry air . . .

. . . we love moist air!

Coconut palm

Cape primrose

Banana plant

friends for a couple of weeks. Plants don't like the smell of fresh paint or turpentine.)

Many plants need not only fresh but moist air. Outside, dew and rain supply plenty of moisture. But inside, it's up to you—especially during the winter, when indoor heating dries up the air. You can spray the leaves directly with water. Or you can put containers of water between the plants, or set your flowerpot right into a dish filled with gravel and water. Plants that need very moist air can even be moved into the bathroom during the winter—but only if there's a window to let in light. Look out for telltale signs that the air is too dry for your plants: leaf tips and edges will turn brown.

Rub-a-dub-dub —
A fern in my tub!

Ways to keep the air moist.

Some Like It Hot, Some Like It Cool

Cactuses come from the hot desert.

Many orchids grow in Japan.

The dragon-tree's home is on the warm Canary Islands.

Plants come from all kinds of different climates: dry, hot deserts; steamy rain forests; and places that have changing seasons (winter, spring, summer, and fall). Indoors, a plant will thrive in the temperature it was used to in its homeland. Of course, no plant can tell you where it comes from and whether it

There! This way I'll remember what my impatiens likes...

warm sunny bright moist

prefers warm or cool surroundings. But a florist or a good plant book can give you this information.

Most plants are happy at ordinary summer temperatures. In winter you'll have to take special care. If plants stand on a cold windowsill or stone floor, they may freeze, even in a heated room. Simply slide a small wood board or a piece of carpet underneath the pot to protect the roots. No plant likes frost on the window on a winter's morning. Move your pots away from windows so that leaves don't touch the glass. If necessary, put a piece of cardboard between the pot and the windowpane during the night. Sometimes these tricks aren't enough to keep every plant warm enough in its usual spot. You may have to move a few (more about this on page 38).

Also, watch out for sudden temperature changes. If you move plants from a warm room to a cool terrace or vice versa, first let them sit in a medium-cool spot (maybe a hallway) for two to three days.

When frost sparkles on the window, protect your plant with a piece of cardboard.

Ferns come from steamy rain forests.

A small wood board or a piece of carpet keeps your plants' feet warm.

Long, thin spouts pour best.

Watering:
Too Much, Too Little,
or Just Right?

How often do you have to water your plants? There's really no one answer—that's why many plants come with a tag that gives watering guidelines. Here are a few general hints:

- Plants need more water during summer.
- You should water more often when the sun shines and less often when it's rainy.
- Plants in small pots need to be watered more often than plants in big ones—but when you do water a plant in a large pot, give it plenty.

When in doubt, just check the dampness of the soil by pressing your thumb into it. If the soil doesn't stick to your thumb, your plant probably needs water.

Once you've decided it's watering time, water your plants with care. In winter they may not like ice-cold tap water; use room-temperature instead. Also, most plants don't like having wet feet. Water your plants until water runs out the bottom of the pot into the saucer, but check the saucer half an hour later and pour off any water that the soil hasn't absorbed. (There's an exception to this rule: the umbrella plant grows

Brrrrrr!
Never use ice-cold water. In winter fill your watering can ahead of time and let it sit so that the water will reach room temperature.

Check the dampness of the soil with your thumb.

Most plants can be watered from above...

but you can water others from below.

This plant has had too much water — or too little!

When you tap on a pot and hear a thudding sound, the soil is moist enough — wait awhile before watering.

naturally in swamps and likes to stand in water even when it's potted.) Most plants can be watered from the top, right into the soil. But plants with a lot of dense leaves, such as baby's tears, are better watered from the bottom: just pour the water into the saucer under the pot.

In most cases you'll notice right away if a plant is not getting enough water: its leaves, twigs, and blossoms will droop, wither, and die. The problem is that plants react the same way if they have had *too much* water.

Why? Because when roots become waterlogged, they can't supply water to the upper part of the plant. Then the upper part dries out while the lower part drowns. So be very careful not to overwater your plants.

If a plant has drowned, nothing will save it. But you may be able to rescue a plant that has completely dried out. Put the whole plant (in its pot) right into a bucket of water until no air bubbles rise up (about 10 minutes). Then take it out and hope for the best!

A cure for a dried-out plant: 10 minutes soaking in water...

Amazing two-tone flowers

EXPERIMENT

You can dye white blossoms with colored ink or water-soluble paint mixed with water. Slit the stem and place each half in a different glass.

15

Plants drinking with string straws!

This pot has a secret water compartment.

Clay pots

gravel

moist soil
or
peat moss

While You're Away . . .

Most plants need regular care. So what happens when you go away for a week or two? If you're lucky, you'll find someone nice enough to water your plants while you're gone. You can leave a note about the special needs of each one. But if you don't have anybody to help you out, don't worry. Arrange for your plants to take care of themselves for a while. Here are some great tricks.

For plants in clay pots, take a big tray or washtub and spread layers of gravel and moist peat moss (or potting soil) in it. Set your plants there so they'll stay moist while you're gone.

You can also build a pipeline of string for plants in plastic pots. Take a piece of thick cotton cord (laundry line is perfect) and wet it. Then bury one end in the soil and drop the other end into a container filled with water (the water level must be higher than the soil level for this to work). The plants will drink water right through the cord!

Another way to keep moisture in is to build a mini-tent for each large plant. The clear plastic bags that come from the cleaners are just right for this. Set the pot down in the bag, and water the plant thoroughly. Then

Nip off buds.

IMPORTANT!

Move plants away from the window while you're gone.

Plants that grow in water (aquatic plants) take care of themselves.

The plastic-bag greenhouse

Great! Everybody's taken care of.

stick a few long stakes into the soil so that the bag doesn't fall onto the leaves, and tie the bag above the plant to keep air from seeping in. Now the water can't evaporate: it'll stay inside the bag and keep your plant moist.

You can also help your plants use less water while you're gone. First, move them away from sunny windows and into shady corners or onto the floor. Then nip off wilted leaves and most of the flower buds—plants without blossoms need less water. As for window boxes or plants on a terrace, water the plants thoroughly just before you

go, and cover the soil with wet sand or wet peat moss. With luck it'll rain while you're away!

Whatever method you decide to use, try it out *before* you go on vacation. Then you'll know for sure how long your plants can get along without you.

17

Something to Grow On: Plant Food

We don't need much food...

Snake plant

Yucca

Ti plant

Most plants need more than light, air, and water in order to grow. They also need plant food, or fertilizer. Fertilizer contains three important ingredients: nitrogen, which helps branches and leaves grow; phosphorus, which gives your plant strong roots and plenty of blossoms; and potassium, which keeps the whole plant healthy.

Plants should be fertilized only during the time they grow and blossom—that's usually from spring to fall. During the winter most plants should rest, or slow down their growth, and they don't need any fertilizer. (See page 38 for more about plants in winter.)

Fertilizer comes in different forms. You can find liquid fertilizers, pellets or spikes to stick in the soil every month, and white grains of slow-release fertilizer to mix with the soil while you're planting or repotting. Every bottle or package will come with its own directions to follow. But it's good to ask a florist for

Please give us plenty!

Hydrangea

Geranium

This Venus flytrap catches its own food — insects!

advice about which fertilizer to buy and how much to use. Plants have different needs. Some will want a portion every week while others are perfectly happy with a little serving once a month. Certain plants—cactuses, for instance—even need special fertilizer.

You can get liquid fertilizer, or little spikes that poke right into the soil.

How can you be sure you're using the right amount of fertilizer? If a plant seems to be growing very slowly, if its stems are thin and its leaves have little color, and if it has hardly any blossoms, it's probably getting too little food. Luckily the plant will recover quickly once you start fertilizing it more often. On the other hand, too *much* fertilizer can harm or even kill your plants. Leaves will change shape and turn brown at the edges, and the soil will be covered with a saltlike crust. Try to save your plant by putting it into fresh soil as

soon as you can or by rinsing out the fertilizer under running water.

A special treat: mineral water!

Be careful when you handle fertilizer. It may leave ugly spots where it touches the leaves of a plant. (Should this happen, wash the leaves immediately with plain water.) One last fertilizing tip: If the soil is dry, water your plant before you fertilize.

If you have to rinse fertilizer off an overfed plant, give it less water for a while.

Peas, mustard, and lupines help fertilize your garden! After they bloom, cut them down and turn them under the soil.

Young plants grow quickly. So once a year, give each one a nice, roomy new pot. When plants get older, they need fresh soil about once every three years. Choose a new pot that's only a little larger than the old one—it should be about two thirds of an inch bigger across. If the pot is too big, the roots will crisscross the soil instead of helping the plant grow new leaves and blossoms.

It doesn't make much difference whether you use clay or plastic pots. All you need to know is that plants in plastic pots need a little less water. But if you have a thick, heavy plant such as a ponytail plant, choose a heavy clay pot, since a lightweight plastic one could tip over easily.

Don't feel you have to stick with plain flowerpots—use your imagination! How about putting a plant in an old cooking pot, an egg cup, a basket, or even an old rubber boot? Whatever you use as a planter, make sure water doesn't collect in the bottom—either put holes in it or add an extra-thick layer of gravel.

Time for a Change: Repotting

Watch out
for cactus needles!
A newspaper will
help you handle
prickly plants.

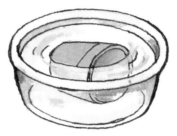

Soak new clay pots
in water for a day.

Any of these
would make a
fine planter!

You can grow a new plant from cuttings.

Get Your Plants into Shape: Pruning

What if your plant grows so tall that it hits the ceiling? Or winds its way all over the room? Don't panic; congratulate yourself on the fine work you've done!

Ivy in water will grow new roots.

Besides, you can always make a plant smaller. Just snip away very carefully with your scissors. Most plants need to be pruned, or trimmed, sometimes—even small and young plants. This helps them grow evenly, with plenty of full, bushy branches. To keep a plant healthy, cut off about an inch or an inch and a half—only at the uppermost tips. Snip right above a leaf (but not *too* close to it).

Keep in mind that you can even use what you cut off to grow a new plant. Stick your cutting right into a pot of damp soil, and it will grow roots. Don't be discouraged if plants don't always grow from cuttings, though. That happens to the best professional gardeners, too!

Trim carefully!

(See page 30 for more about cuttings.) After trimming, plants need special care. Spray the leaves with water often during the following weeks. And if your plant looks terrible during the first few days, don't worry. Soon it will be healthier and happier than it was before.

Pruning plants with hard or woody branches, such as ficus trees and rubber plants, can be difficult. Instead of hacking away at them, try a trick professionals use. It's a way of pruning an old plant and starting a new one at the same time. The pictures on

A well-rounded boxwood

the right show you how. With an adult's help, use a sharp knife to cut halfway into the stem. Then wedge a pebble or toothpick into the opening to keep it from growing together again (1). Below this point, tie some plastic wrap around the stem so that it forms a little bag. Stuff some moist peat or sphagnum moss into it (most garden centers sell sphagnum moss, a stringy, grayish substance that's great for rooting plants) (2). Tie the bag closed on top (3). After about six weeks roots will have grown where you cut into the plant. Slice off the top and plant it in a new pot (4). Now you have *two* plants!

How about experimenting when you trim? Give a boxwood plant a special shape, or make a geranium or rosemary into a small tree (this project will take a year or two).

Pruning can turn one plant into two!

EXPERIMENT

Make a plant into a tree!
First year: Cut the side branches.
Second year: Trim the top.

Ahhh! Now I can breathe again!

Spring Cleaning

Wipe large leaves with a wet sponge.

As time goes on, dirt collects on the leaves of any plant, clogging up the pores, or tiny openings, that take in fresh air and moisture. So set aside a plant-cleaning day once a year. Not only will your plants be healthier when they're free of dirt, but they'll look better, too.

A lukewarm shower over the bathtub will clean small plants with firm leaves, but don't make the shower too heavy! Wash really large plants leaf by leaf with a soft sponge and plain water. A soft, dry paintbrush is best for dusting plants with hairy leaves, such as African violets. Their leaves must never get wet.

If during cleaning you find that some of your plants have weak stems, put long stakes into their pots to support them. Be careful not to tie a plant too tightly to its stake, though: it needs space to keep on growing.

Suppose you have a philodendron or another vine that's growing wild, taking up more than its share of space. You might decide to prune it, but you can also neaten it up by supporting its rambling tendrils with a special moss stake. When you attach the vine to the stake, it will grow extra roots in the moss. These aerial roots will help the plant grow tall and strong instead

Pinch off faded leaves and blossoms.

Small plants like a gentle shower.

Extra support for vines: A roll of wire mesh... is stuffed with sphagnum moss from the garden center. Put plant and stake in a pot of soil... and fasten shoots with wire so that roots can grow into the stake.

of long and scraggly. (See the pictures and directions for making a moss stake.) Remember to spray the stake with water every time you water the base of the plant.

How about turning a climbing plant into a leafy mouse or rabbit? With a little practice, you can make all kinds of green figures. Carefully bend wire mesh to form a simple shape such as an arch, a heart, or an animal. (You'll have an easier time if you pick an animal without long legs!) Stuff the figure with sphagnum moss (see page 23) the same way you stuff a moss stake, and put it in your plant's pot. Then wind the tendrils around the shape, fastening them with wire. To cover the figure completely with creepers, you'll need to use climbing plants with small leaves—try ivy, creeping fig, or jasmine.

You can support your outdoor plants with stakes too.

Bug Off!
Getting Rid of Plant Pests

Just like us, plants can get sick. You can tell your plants are ailing if they get ugly spots, their leaves hang down or turn yellow, and they don't want to grow anymore.

Sometimes this happens if they're not getting the right amount of light or water. You can fix these problems easily enough.

But sometimes there's a more serious problem: bugs. Aphids, mealybugs, and other tiny insects suck the sap from the branches and leaves. And when a plant loses all its sap and strength, it dies. If you discover the pests in time and drive them away, your plant will be just fine.

About once a week, make a pest check. First look underneath the leaves, where insects love to hide. Sticky spots on the windowsill are a sign of insect visitors, as are spotted leaves, brown leaf tips, or curling leaf edges.

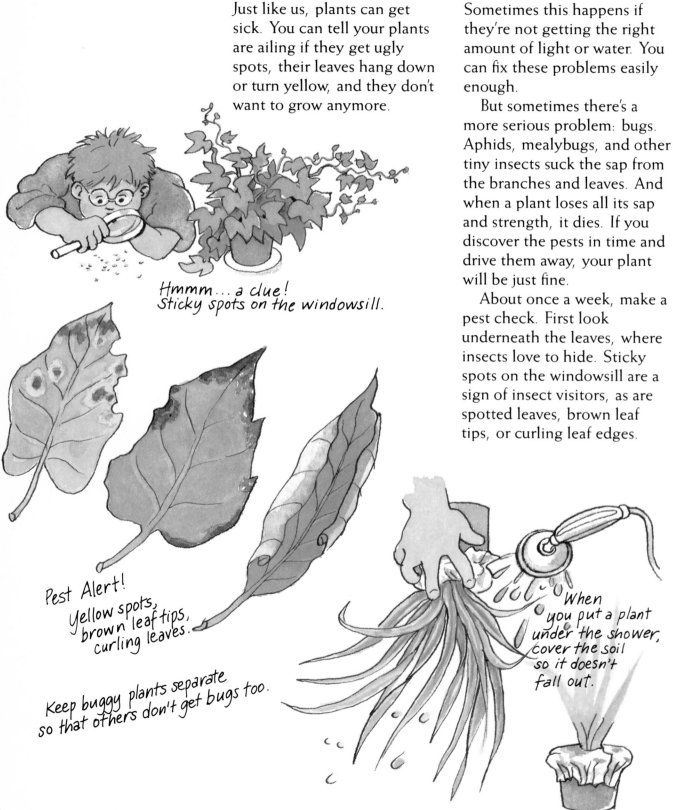

Hmmm...a clue!
Sticky spots on the windowsill.

Pest Alert!
Yellow spots, brown leaf tips, curling leaves.

Keep buggy plants separate so that others don't get bugs too.

When you put a plant under the shower, cover the soil so it doesn't fall out.

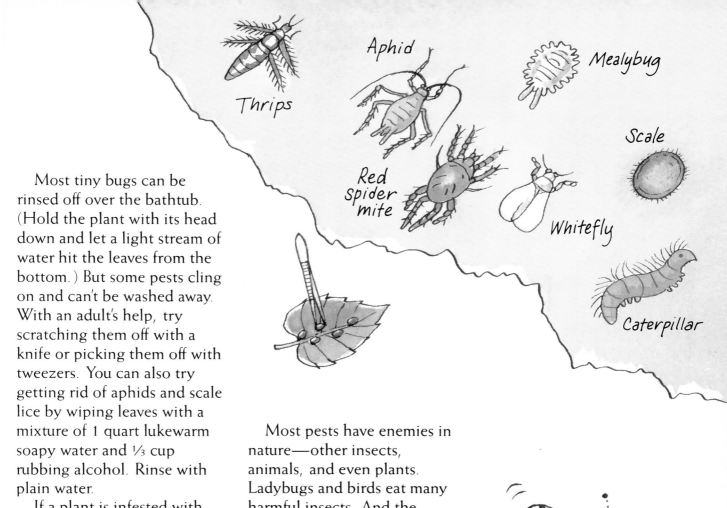

Thrips

Aphid

Mealybug

Scale

Red spider mite

Whitefly

Caterpillar

Most tiny bugs can be rinsed off over the bathtub. (Hold the plant with its head down and let a light stream of water hit the leaves from the bottom.) But some pests cling on and can't be washed away. With an adult's help, try scratching them off with a knife or picking them off with tweezers. You can also try getting rid of aphids and scale lice by wiping leaves with a mixture of 1 quart lukewarm soapy water and ⅓ cup rubbing alcohol. Rinse with plain water.

If a plant is infested with aphids from top to bottom, you might have to turn to store-bought pesticides. Look for sprays and dips made from all-natural ingredients. You'll also see chemical pesticides, but since they're not always safe for you or for the environment, steer clear of them.

Most pests have enemies in nature—other insects, animals, and even plants. Ladybugs and birds eat many harmful insects. And the smells of garlic, lavender, and marigolds will drive most pests away; plant these as guards for your flowers, vegetables, and even potted plants. Some people say that spraying or watering with a mixture of water and hot peppers or garlic will keep bugs at a distance too.

Take caterpillars to the woods or park. They'll turn into butterflies!

You can scratch off some pests, but ask an adult to help.

Seed sowing made simple: try seed tape!

SEED STARTING MIX

Where It All Begins: Planting Seeds

Planting seeds step by step:

Fill a box with soil.

Smooth the soil.

Drop the seeds on top in regular rows.

Cover with a very thin layer of soil.

Moisten with a spray bottle.

Cover the box loosely with plastic wrap...

then put it in a warm place.

The soil should never dry up — spray it occasionally.

When you see green tips, remove the plastic.

All plants—from the tallest trees to the tiniest flowers—grow from seeds. Where do seeds come from? Plants! Maybe you've noticed seeds in the center of flowers or fruits. You may be able to grow plants from these seeds, but you'll have the best luck planting seeds you buy. They are sold in small packets or on special seed tape at supermarkets, five-and-tens, and plant nurseries. (A list of places for ordering seeds and other supplies is on page 43.)

Most seeds can be planted in a mixture of coarse sand and fine peat moss or in a special seed starting mix that you can buy. You can start plants in a flowerpot, a box, a flat dish, an egg carton, or an empty yogurt cup. Remember, for most plants, spring is the best sowing time. If you have seeds left

The largest seed in the world: a coconut!

over after planting, store them in a small paper bag in a dark place until next year. Or why not try setting up a plant swap with your friends? Each of you can sow one kind of seed and then you can trade baby plants.

You'd be surprised how strong seeds are. Try this experiment with a dried bean (which is a seed) to find out just how much power they have. Stir half a cup of powdered plaster into some water to form a paste. Pour it into a paper cup, and stick in the dried bean. When the paste is dry, pull off the cup and put the hardened plaster plug in a saucer filled with water. Wait and see what happens!

Now my plants need more space!

Gently lift the seedlings out with a spoon.

Separate them carefully...

and plant three or four in a flowerpot. A pencil makes neat holes.

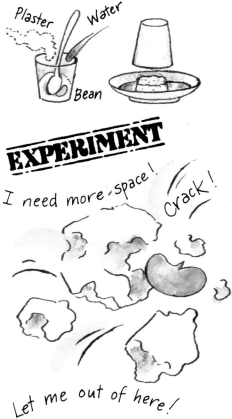

Plaster   Water
Bean

EXPERIMENT

I need more space!   Crack!

Let me out of here!

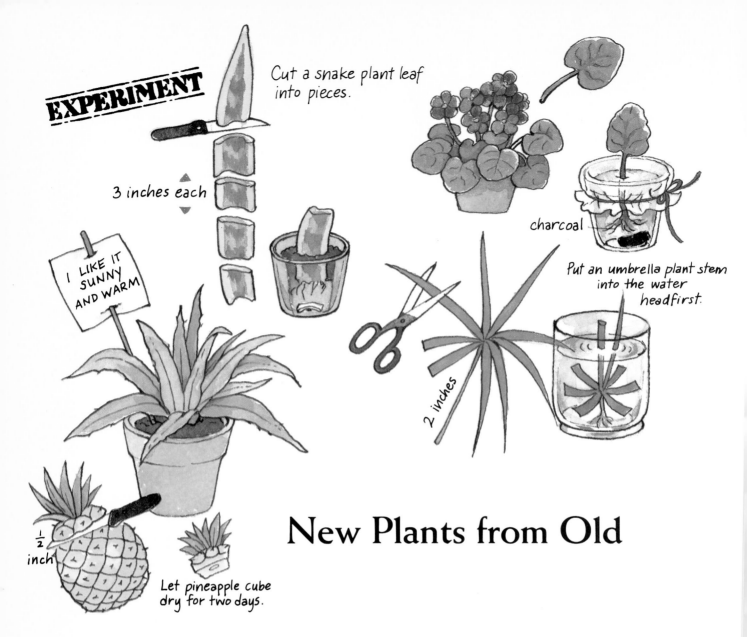

Cut a snake plant leaf into pieces.

3 inches each

charcoal

Put an umbrella plant stem into the water headfirst.

I LIKE IT SUNNY AND WARM

2 inches

½ inch

Let pineapple cube dry for two days.

New Plants from Old

All around you there are plants just waiting to grow— not only from seeds, but from scraps of old plants and even from kitchen leftovers! Here's an experiment with a pineapple. Save the top with its spiky leaves, making sure that a little over half an inch of the fruit is still attached to it. Trim all around so that only a cube of fruit and the leaves are left. Let the cube dry for two days, and then bury it in a mixture of peat and coarse sand. With a little luck, the cut-off leaves will grow roots and become a new pineapple!

You can grow new plants in the same way from the tops of turnips, radishes, carrots, and red beets. (Unfortunately, a carrot or turnip forest won't live very long and won't give you any new vegetables.) A sweet potato will make quite a spectacular leafy plant. First, stick three toothpicks in the center of the potato and hang it in a glass of water. When roots appear, you can pot the potato, letting a little bit of it come out of the soil. Soon it will grow into an ivylike plant with yard-long shoots.

Here's another experiment that's practically guaranteed to work. Cut off a stem from an umbrella plant. Then stick the stem headfirst into a glass of water (you may have to trim both the leaves and the stem to make it fit). New

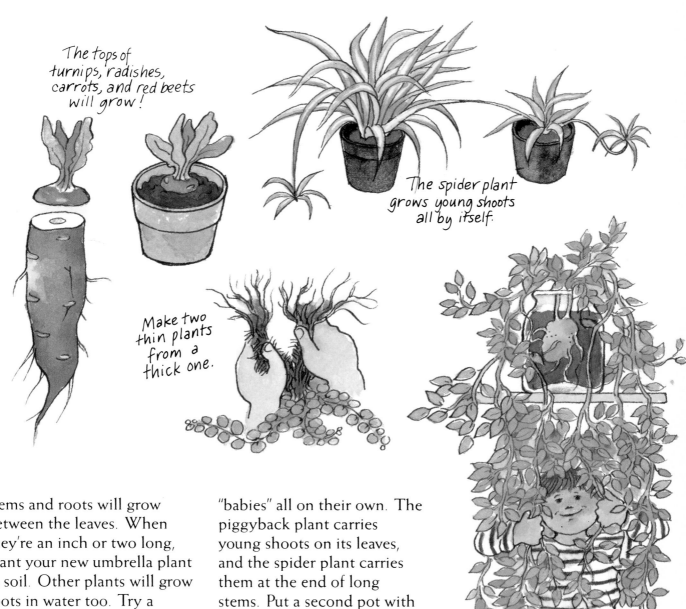

The tops of turnips, radishes, carrots, and red beets will grow!

The spider plant grows young shoots all by itself.

Make two thin plants from a thick one.

stems and roots will grow between the leaves. When they're an inch or two long, plant your new umbrella plant in soil. Other plants will grow roots in water too. Try a single leaf from an African violet or a shoot of ivy. Hint: Throw a piece of charcoal into the water—it will cut down on bacteria that eat away at the stems.

Sometimes you can make several small plants from one big one. When you repot a thick fern or another plant that has a lot of stems poking out of the soil, tear it into clumps (ask an adult to help you cut really thick roots) and pot each one separately.

Other plants start growing "babies" all on their own. The piggyback plant carries young shoots on its leaves, and the spider plant carries them at the end of long stems. Put a second pot with soil next to the mother plant, fasten the baby plant onto the pot with a piece of florist's wire, and it will take root. Then you can cut off the stem and enjoy the new arrival.

Here's one last fun thing to try: Make four or five new plants from a single leaf of a snake plant. Just cut one of the long, fleshy leaves horizontally into several pieces. Stick each piece, bottom edge down, into soil. New plants will grow from the edges!

My sweet potato— isn't it a beauty?

The Terrace Garden

If you have a terrace or porch, you're in luck. It's a great place to try out all kinds of wonderful garden projects. How about planting a butterfly lawn? You can buy a special mix of seeds to grow the grasses and flowers that butterflies love, and your garden will be aflutter with butterflies all summer long. You can also try growing a forest in a large pail. Simply stick a few acorns, beechnuts, or chestnuts into the soil. Let them sit through a winter in the pail—and who knows? You could end up with a mighty oak someday!

If you have a cat, sow a little lawn for it in a box. Just follow the directions on the seed package, and the grass should shoot up in a few weeks. Cats love to nibble on fresh grass—and it's very good for them.

Here are a few more ideas for fixing up your terrace. Use a washtub to make a lily pond, complete with a small cattail or two. Attach a birdbath to the railing to invite feathered visitors. Make a desert oasis in a sandbox with some tiny palm trees. For a real treat, grow a pumpkin-in-a-pot: you'll have blossoms in the summer and pumpkins in the fall!

A jungle for your cat

Your own personal forest

A swimming pool
for birds

A
desert
oasis

Be a Fifth-Floor Farmer

Suppose you want a vegetable garden but you don't have a backyard. Don't worry—you can become a farmer on a terrace or even on an indoor windowsill, as long as it gets some sun. Growing herbs and vegetables in boxes and pots takes a little work, of course, but it'll be worth it. Try to water every day.

Fertilizing is also important: vegetables need to be fed every week, herbs about every second or third week.

You can plant vegetables and herbs yourself from seeds, starting in March or

Dig out those zucchini recipes—this vegetable grows like crazy!

April. From the middle of May on, small starter plants will appear in stores and outdoor markets, and you can simply repot these in larger containers.

Almost anything will grow on a terrace, from corn to gooseberry bushes. But it's better to start with easy-care crops—herbs, radishes, lettuce, strawberries, and zucchini. For windowsills, herbs, tomatoes, and

Yum! Fresh Vegetables from your own garden!

RADISHES

three sprouting eyes in each piece. Let the cut pieces dry for a day or two. Then bury them completely in a bucket of moist soil about six inches deep. As soon as you see sprouts above ground, move the bucket to the terrace. Wait till the green shoots are about four inches high, and then pack more soil on top of them. Repeat this process until you reach the top of the bucket. This way the potatoes will form extra-long roots, and the longer the roots, the more potatoes you'll get! Harvest your potatoes in fall when the leaves turn yellow.

strawberries will work better than leafier plants like lettuce and zucchini.

Growing potatoes in a bucket is fun and fairly easy. And since potatoes grow underground, harvesting them is like digging for treasure. Find two small potatoes with lots of eyes that are beginning to sprout (most potatoes sprout if they're just left alone for two weeks). Cut them into pieces with one to

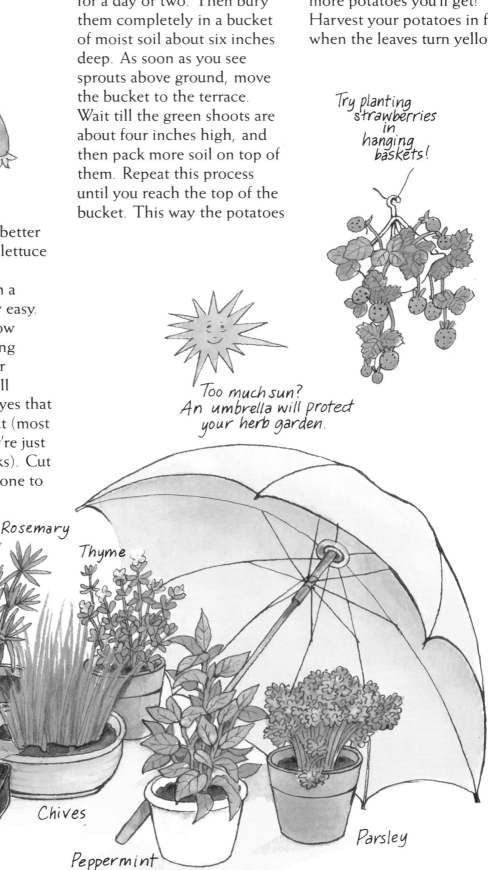

Try planting strawberries in hanging baskets!

Too much sun? An umbrella will protect your herb garden.

Rosemary

Thyme

Sage

Chives

Basil

Peppermint

Parsley

Your Little Corner of the World

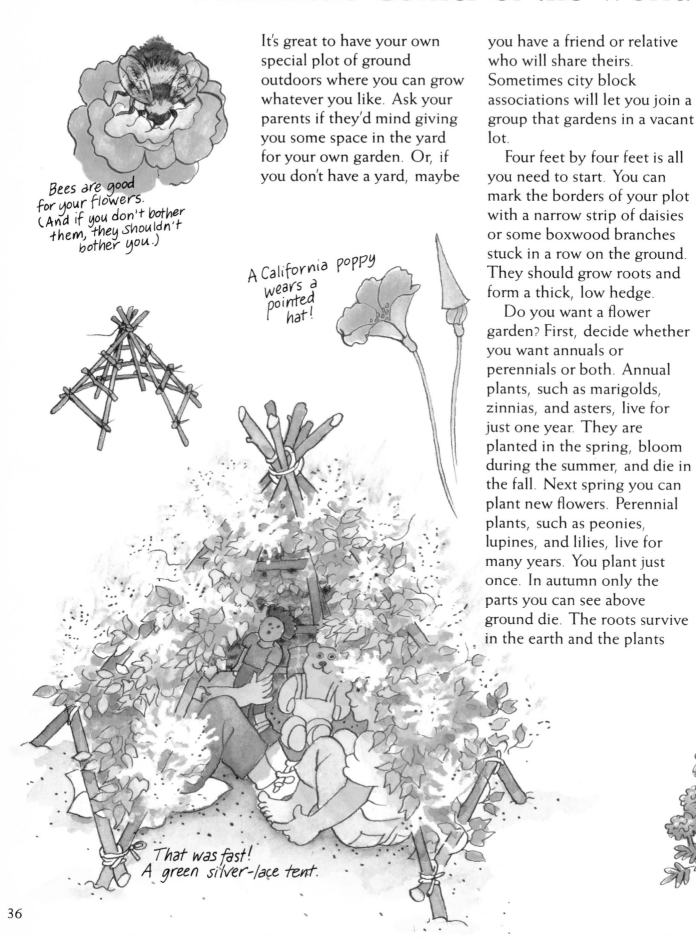

Bees are good for your flowers. (And if you don't bother them, they shouldn't bother you.)

A California poppy wears a pointed hat!

That was fast! A green silver-lace tent.

It's great to have your own special plot of ground outdoors where you can grow whatever you like. Ask your parents if they'd mind giving you some space in the yard for your own garden. Or, if you don't have a yard, maybe you have a friend or relative who will share theirs. Sometimes city block associations will let you join a group that gardens in a vacant lot.

Four feet by four feet is all you need to start. You can mark the borders of your plot with a narrow strip of daisies or some boxwood branches stuck in a row on the ground. They should grow roots and form a thick, low hedge.

Do you want a flower garden? First, decide whether you want annuals or perennials or both. Annual plants, such as marigolds, zinnias, and asters, live for just one year. They are planted in the spring, bloom during the summer, and die in the fall. Next spring you can plant new flowers. Perennial plants, such as peonies, lupines, and lilies, live for many years. You plant just once. In autumn only the parts you can see above ground die. The roots survive in the earth and the plants

Making perfume
EXPERIMENT

Mix a small amount of rubbing alcohol (90%) with the same quantity of distilled water.

Cut fragrant flowers into pieces and soak them in the mixture for two days.

Pour the mixture through a strainer and put it into a pretty bottle.

My perfume

sprout up again and again every spring.

Planting your own private patch of velvety lawn might be fun too. Just be prepared to mow every week during the summer! A flower garden needs different care. You have to keep the beds free of weeds and pinch off wilted blossoms so that your flowers can grow new buds. Water once a week if it hasn't rained (or every day if you live in a very dry climate).

Maybe your garden plot is large enough for a green tent. If it is, just stick a few stakes slanting toward each other in the ground (see the picture), tie them together in the middle, and fasten a few

crosspieces between them. Plant some silver-lace vine next to every second stake. It should grow very quickly, and soon you'll have a secret hideout.

It's mowing day!

I like *long* grass!

ENGLISH DAISIES

A Winter's Rest for Your Plants

Ideal winter temperature: 60 degrees F.

Certain animals, like woodchucks, ground squirrels, and some bears, hibernate—they spend the cold months of winter resting. Most outdoor plants take a rest in the winter too. Trees lose their leaves, and the upper parts of perennial plants wither and die. In the spring they start to grow again.

Most indoor plants also need to slow down their growth for a while. They need to collect strength for blooming and growing in the coming year. If they're never given a chance to rest, they may hold out for a few years, but they're apt to die sooner than normal. So don't encourage your plants to grow in the winter—water them less often and don't fertilize them at all. Try to keep your plants in a cool place, at a temperature of

Winter watering: Just give your plant a little water when it shrivels.

about 60 degrees Fahrenheit (F), during the winter months.

Some plants like to rest at lower temperatures—41 to 47 degrees F—which makes your job a little more complicated. Your geranium, fuchsia, and begonia would be happiest in a dark, damp basement. Cut back the green stalks and store the roots and soil until spring. The hardiest plants, such as a rosebush, a bamboo, or silver-lace in a bucket, are best left outside

Turn the radiator down.

Here's a warm winter coat!

The bulb already contains a new flower.

on the porch or terrace during the winter. Wrap them well so that they won't freeze! First slide a piece of wood or carpet under the bucket to prevent cold feet; then wind layers of newspaper or wrapping material around the bucket. If you make a mound of extra soil in the pot, a normal winter won't harm your plant.

Another winter project: Plant some spring flowers to bloom in time for Christmas. Hyacinth and paper-white narcissus bulbs are the easiest to grow. Just put them in a glass or bowl filled with water and gravel, and follow the directions next to the pictures on the right.

Winter narcissus!

Buy pre-cooled narcissus bulbs at your garden center. Put a layer of gravel in a dish, add water, and set the bulbs in, points up. Keep the dish on a sunny windowsill. Wait 4-5 weeks for flowers.

Begonias winter best in the basement.

Place a hyacinth bulb in a glass of water and cover with a little paper hat. Keep it in a cool spot the first 8 weeks, then move it to a very warm place.

A geranium's year

Plant seeds in January.

In May transfer plants to window boxes.

Water and fertilize them often during the summer.

In August start some new plants.

In September or October take the plants out of the boxes.

Cut back stalks that are too long.

During the winter keep the plants in a box in the basement.

In February or March move them back to a warm, bright place.

Choices! Choices!

Now that you know how to grow and care for plants, it's time to get started! On these pages you'll find a sampling of plants to choose from—tall or small, delicate, lush, spiky, green or multicolored . . . it's up to you. But don't be disappointed if you can't find some of these at your florist or nursery. There are many, many kinds of plants to discover. Good luck and good growing!

Euphorbia

Coleus

Fern

Bamboo

Agave

Persian violet

Caladium

Swiss cheese plant

Amaryllis

Snake plant

Dragon tree

Balfour aralia

Pineapple

Browallia

Cape primrose

Flamingo flower

Venus flytrap

Baby's tears

Ivy

Boxwood

Ponytail plant

Banana plant

Impatiens

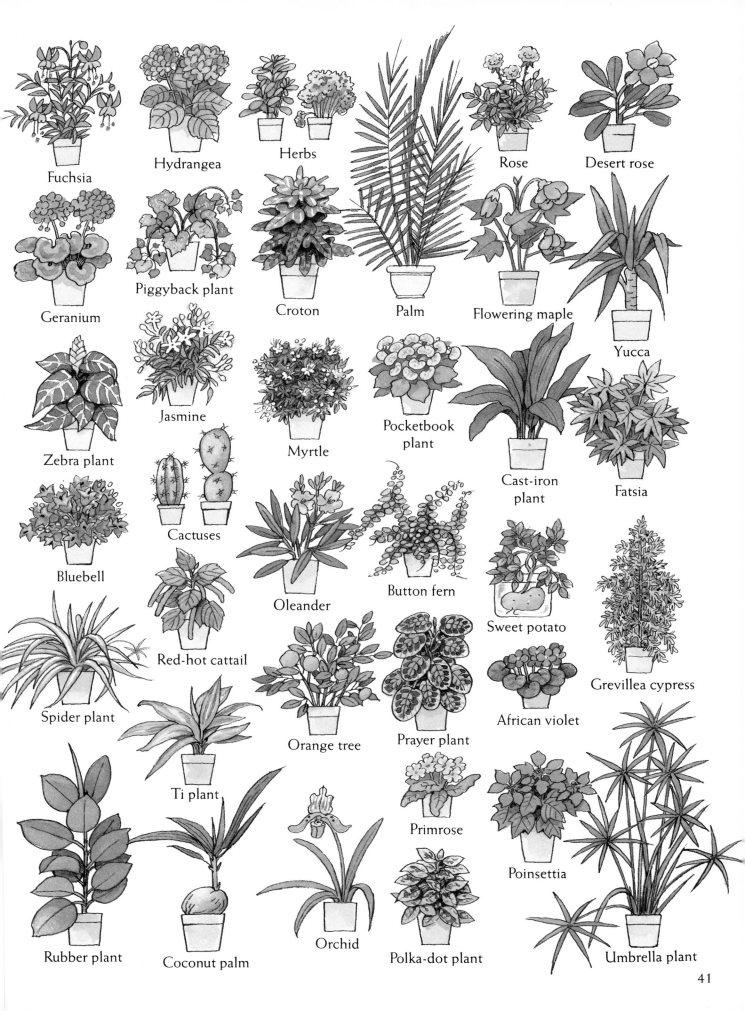

Fuchsia

Hydrangea

Herbs

Rose

Desert rose

Geranium

Piggyback plant

Croton

Palm

Flowering maple

Yucca

Zebra plant

Jasmine

Myrtle

Pocketbook plant

Cast-iron plant

Fatsia

Bluebell

Cactuses

Oleander

Button fern

Sweet potato

Grevillea cypress

Spider plant

Red-hot cattail

Orange tree

Prayer plant

African violet

Ti plant

Primrose

Poinsettia

Rubber plant

Coconut palm

Orchid

Polka-dot plant

Umbrella plant

41

FINDING WHAT YOU NEED

You can probably find a good garden center in your neighborhood. But you can also order seeds, bulbs, tools, and other supplies by mail. The companies listed below all have catalogs, and most of them are free. Just write and ask for one. (You'll be more likely to find seeds that will grow well in your area if you order from a store in or near your own state.)

Look for fun offerings like special starter kits for kids, seed mixes for just a penny, "meadows in a can," butterfly gardens, and packets of seeds for growing tiny pumpkins, cotton, or yard-long beans!

Allen, Sterling, & Lothrop
191 U.S. Rte. 1
Falmouth, ME 04105

W. Atlee Burpee Company
300 Park Avenue
Warminster, PA 18974

D. V. Burrell Seed Growers Company
P.O. Box 150
Rocky Ford, CO 81067

Henry Field Seed & Nursery Company
Shenandoah, IA 51602

Garden-Ville
6266 Highway 290 West
Austin, TX 78735

Glasshouse Works
Church Street
P.O. Box 97
Stewart, OH 45778-0097

Gurney's Seed & Nursery Company
110 Capitol St.
Yankton, SD 57079

Harris Seeds
60 Saginaw Dr.
Rochester, NY 14623

H. G. Hastings Company
P.O. Box 115535
Atlanta, GA 30310

High Altitude Gardens
P.O. Box 4619
Ketchum, ID 83340

J. L. Hudson, Seedsman
P.O. Box 1058
Redwood City, CA 94064

J. W. Jung Seed Company
335 South High St.
Randolph, WI 53957

Logee's Greenhouses
141 North St.
Danielson, CT 06239

Earl May Seed & Nursery Company
208 North Elm
Shenandoah, IA 51603

Mellingers
2310 South Range Rd.
North Lima, OH 44452

Natural Gardening Supply Co.
217 San Anselmo Ave.
San Anselmo, CA 94960

George W. Park Seed Company
Highway 254 North
P.O. Box 31
Greenwood, SC 29647

Porter & Son, Seedsman
P.O. Box 104
Stephenville, TX 76401

Roswell Seed Company
P.O. Box 725
Roswell, NM 88202

Shepherd's Garden Seeds
30 Irene St.
Torrington, CT 06790

INDEX

ABOUT THE AUTHOR

Plant wizard ERIKA MARKMANN is a freelance magazine journalist and the author of several noted gardening books for adults. Her German edition of *Grow It!* won the prestigious German Society for Garden Design Book Award in 1989. She and her husband have a "huge garden and countless potted plants."

ABOUT THE ILLUSTRATOR

GISELA KÖNEMUND illustrates and writes nonfiction books for children when she's not painting pictures for magazines and advertisements. Her illustrations for this book reflect her wide knowledge and love of plants. She lives in Hamburg, Germany, with her husband and two children.